I0480477

Goal Setting Workshop

How To Set Effective Goals And Achieve MASSIVE SUCCESS In All Areas Of Life

Alex Silva

Copyright © 2020 Alex Silva.

All rights reserved

No part of this book may be reproduced, or stored in a retrieval system, or transmitted in any form or by any means, electronic, mechanical, photocopying, recording, or otherwise, without express written permission of the publisher.

Get the free "5 Habits of Self-Made Millionaires" at:

Thealexsilva.com

Why I Wrote This Book

After years of setting various goals and never achieving them, I decided to study all traditional and modern goal-setting techniques.

I read and studied hundreds of self-help books, courses, and information from the world wide web specifically in the area of goal setting.

Then I decided to create my own technique that compiles the best of traditional goal-setting and the modern goal-setting techniques including techniques of pseudoscience's. You will learn an Eight-step Goal Achievement Blueprint.

I wrote this book so that people can take advantage of all the resources of the world and utilize them in their own personal life, without taking years of trial and error.

Why You Should Read

This Book

Setting goals is building a successful path in your life. Setting goals is planning your future in advance and developing the necessary skills to achieve success.

Not only does setting goals has shown to increase levels of motivation, but it also can affect our emotions too.

I usually say that the price of excellence is ten thousand hours (Yes, 10 000).

Think of the thousands of hours of research time you will save by reading this book. You certainly could do the research yourself and come up with an effective goal-setting strategy, but you don't have to. I did the research for you so that you cut short your learning curve and achieve success way faster because time is limited. From the day we are born we have a limited time to live, get the edge over life!

You can see this book can be worth thousands or even hundreds of thousands of dollars. Don't waste your time. Read it!

Table of Contents

Chapter 1. Introduction

First of all, I wanted to start by congratulating you.

Congratulations for buying this book, this tells me that you are the type of person that is committed to invest your time and energy to achieve your dream goals, and it is that same type of commitment that will allow you to produce tremendous results in your life.

I would like to teach you my own blueprint that you can use in such a way that it will occur on an unconscious level.

You see, the greatest leaders throughout all time have been visionaries, people that have a vision and had the ability to turn their passions into realities.

Give Your Best, And You Will Get the Best

I believe in this simple rule of life, 'you must give to receive'. I found out that my ability to set goals came from many books and all the information that I focused on. There are hundreds, thousands, or even millions of people that read the exact same books, read all the information that I read and never got the results that they want. It's not the books, it's not the seminars, it's not the information, it's all about making it work. For you to achieve excellence, you have to put excellence to obtain excellence (confusing, right?), what I'm saying is that there is no free lunch in this world, there is no miracle until we make it one!

So, I want you to read this book like your life depends on it, even better, I want you to read and apply all the concepts like if your loved one's life was at risk. The following concepts cannot change your life. You are the only one who can.

Before you read this book, I want you to keep this in mind:

There are basically four types of mindsets that people adopt in the way they read books. The first category of people has this resistant or opposing attitude that 'It won't work'. 'I have read other self-help books before and it hasn't worked', or they say, 'It is just another goal setting book'. They adopt this attitude of rejection. When you adopt the attitude of resistance, your brain automatically deletes every open door there is to learn, therefore the value of the book is 0.

Then you have the second category of people who start reading with the attitude of 'let's see if there is anything interesting'. These are the people who will read the book passively, skipping all the exercises, or even avoiding the tasks and adopting a 'let's see if there are any interesting ideas' stance. Unfortunately, while these readers may be entertained while reading or even become aware of some good ideas, they will not do anything about it.

The third category read with the attitude 'let's give it a try, It could have something good'. These people will read the book and try out some of the exercises that interest them, but never with full focus. But that is just about all they do. Do they get anything out of the book? Nine out of ten don't get anything.

Then you have the last and final category. The people who read with the attitude of 'I'm giving this book my one hundred percent' 'I'm taking one hundred percent responsibility for my life'. They read the book, underline the key concepts, and constantly refer to what they have learned. They do the exercises diligently and take each idea into their lives and work on it consistently. These are the people who create a significant change in the results they produce in their lives. When you give your one hundred percent to whatever you do in life you create excellence, let me give you a quick example, have you ever done an exercise or some task where you were one hundred percent committed and focused and everything flowed in the right direction? Exactly, this is what happens when you decide that it is a MUST and you give your one hundred percent

So, before moving on to the next chapter, I want you to make a decision (and really say to yourself) to be 100% committed. Do whatever it takes to finish this book and apply what you learn, and I will guarantee that your life will flow in the direction that you want.

Chapter 2. The Power of Goal Setting

Believe it or not, we all have goals, we all have desires, but why are 90% of people always unhappy and unable to reach their goals?

In 1953 at Yale University, there was a study just before they graduated, and they asked them 'how many of you have a specific set of goals with a plan?' only 3% had their goals written down. Twenty years later, a follow-up study revealed that the 3% of students who wrote down their goals were happier with their marriage, happier with their life in general, more energized, and the really interesting thing was that these three percent earned a combined income three times greater than the combined income of the 97% that had no goals written down.

What is Goal Setting?

Think of it has a roadmap of your success, the destiny of your life. You have the capability to design or redesign your life, take this as the beginning of a new chapter in your life.

Take the example of author Stephen King….

Stephen King that today sold more than 400 million copies of his books was once living in a trailer with his wife, broke and desperate, King received so many rejections that he started to collect them. In his book ON WRITING, he recalls: "By the time I was 14...the nail in my wall would no longer support the weight of the rejection slips impaled upon it. I replaced the nail with a spike and kept on writing.". He received more than 60 rejections before selling his first story. Now, after 60 rejections how do you think Stephen King felt? I bet he felt hopeless and miserable, did he give up? NO, why? Simple, he had a clear vision and a clear plan, until than vision wasn't achieved, he would not stop. Eventually he became one of the world's known writers.

One of my Favorites, Anthony Robbins

From a janitor to a millionaire, you have probably heard about the motivational speaker, Tony Robbins, personally the story of Tony got me so inspired, it made me realize that NOTHING IS IMPOSSIBLE.

Anthony Robbins was raised in a poor family, his mother was addicted to drugs, alcohol and was physically abusive, at the age of 17 he worked as a janitor in a school, after spending every dime that he had he eventually linked up with Jim Rohn, the self-help Guru, where he had given a chance of appearing in stage. After working hard and reading as many books as he could so that he could succeed in public speaking, Tony started working on his own books and programs, which are world-known. Becoming a self-made millionaire.

'Setting goals is the very first step in turning the invisible into the visible' Tony Robbins

Chapter 3. How the

human mind operates

All of us, neurologically, have about 100 Billion neurons (Give or take a few Billion), besides people who are born with severe brain damage or physical disabilities in their brain, all of us have got very similar hardware's.

You may think: "So what? What do I care if all of us have the same capability?

I often hear people say 'He must be a very smart person to achieve that or he had luck or something similar to this'. The success of a person has little or nothing to do with luck (whether you believe in luck or not).

For example, Bill Gates, Jeff Bezos and Warren Buffet, they have the same capability that any human being has, so can you say that you want to be the next Bill Gates or anyone that inspires you? ABSOLUTELY, it's only a matter of strategy, belief, and commitment.

So, if someone is able to do something to their brains, like get themselves motivated or to be able to think in a certain way is because of, not the number of neurons they have, but rather the type of neuro-connection they have created in their brains.

Neuro-connections start to form after twenty weeks after conception. Neuro-connections determine the kind of thought patterns and the kind of behavior we have. Of course, the more connection you have, the smarter you are in a particular area.

Why are some people good in some subjects and others not? For example, if you are good at quantitative thinking and analytical thinking you're probably good at math, that's because in the course of your life you developed a lot of neuro-connections that allow you to understand all of the skills. At the same time, you may not be very good at managing people or art or any other thing, and the reason is the same, you don't have enough neuro-connections. This is what we call neuro-network patterns. It doesn't mean that you can't develop the number of neuro-connections, by practicing and investing your time, day by day you certainly will increase the number of neuro-connections.

It's like driving a car, in the beginning everything seemed complicated, you have to look at your mirrors, at the same time you need to turn on your blinkers while looking at the road, what about now? We do it effortlessly, we increased the number of neuro-connection. Of course, this is a trial and error approach.

What if I told you that you could accelerate dramatically the process of building effective neuro-connections? The process is called modeling (you will use it in one of the eight steps).

For example, if you wanted to learn how to play soccer and you didn't know anything about it, it may take you a while for you to be able to get the techniques and all the necessary skills, in other words, It would take time to create the necessary thought patterns and the neuro-connections to produce that result. Through the process of modeling, we can find someone who is really good at playing soccer, and then we can learn how does he mentally wire his brain to produce the results that we want. We elicit the person's strategy and install it within ourselves so that we can cut short all those years of trial and error.

If we replicate a person's mental blueprint, we can replicate their success, imagine this, if we could replicate the way they think, the way they behave, the way they carry themselves, we can produce the same results they produce. If you were to practice with Cristiano Ronaldo, and you knew how he trains, how he thinks, what is he thinking while playing, you could replicate his success. Now, would you be Cristiano Ronaldo? Of course not, he has years and years of experience, but one thing is for sure, you would be able to shorten your learning curve massively.

Let's take another example, public speaking. Public speaking is the number one fear in the world, so wouldn't it be great if you could walk on stage and deliver a speech with ease and confidence? Guess what, you can.

This concept was developed by two gentlemen, Dr. Richard Bandler and Dr. John Grinder, they decided to study and model people who are excellent in changing people's lives and behaviors.

They modeled people who were master communicators, hypnotist, and many others. They modeled people like Milton Erickson (psychiatrist and psychologist that specialized in medical hypnosis and family therapy), Fritz Pearls (psychiatrist, psychoanalyst, and psychotherapist) and they also modeled Virginia Satir who was the mother of family therapy. It was the beginning of N.L.P (Neuro-Linguistic Programming).

Chapter 4. The 4 Steps of

Modeling

These are the four to effective modeling, in the eight-step goal achievement blueprint we will put this into practice.

Step 1- Identify a model of excellence

Step 2- Observe how this person moves, breathes (deep or shallow?), behaves, gestures (Big gestures or small gestures? Fast or slow gestures?). Observe how he uses his posture, observe his tone of voice (high or low pitch? Fast or slow? raspy or clear?) observe is facial expressions (facial tension or relaxed?)

Step 3 – Image in your mind what would it be like to be this person, step in the shoes of this person, and mentally rehearse. How would you react to the events in your personal life if you were him/her? How would you move, breathe, walk, act, behave, speak?

Step 4 – Physically do it. Become this person, getting the same results he's getting, mimic his physiology, and really associate. Most importantly have fun doing this.

Chapter 5. What do you want?

As you go through this book, I want you really grasp the concepts and start asking yourself, 'What do I want in my life? What do I really want to achieve and create?' 'what's missing in my life?'

Sounds simple right? However, I can tell you that majority of people don't know what they really want, they are just cruising along in the journey of life. I found out that people will most likely say things along the lines of, 'I want to be happy; I want more money, I want a new car, I want to have a perfect relationship'.

Don't get me wrong, there is absolutely nothing wrong with that, in fact, we all want these things, the problem with these "wants" is that they are not specific enough to be achievable.

You see, your brain is like a computer, if you don't give a set of specific instructions, it will stay in the same frame forever, just like your life. After giving it a specific command, the computer will execute in the shortest time possible to achieve the outcome, exactly like your brain.

When you set goals properly your amygdala (the part of the brain that creates emotions) evaluates the degree to which the goal is important to you. Next, your prefrontal cortex (Controls the will power) defines the specifics of what the goal entails. Finally, while knowing your desired goal, your amygdala, and prefrontal cortex work together to keep you focused on moving towards your goals. They also evaluate different scenarios to support your outcome.

This entire process can be grouped into a new study that the scientific community now terms: neuroplasticity (which is the brain's ability to change throughout its lifetime). Surely shows the power of goal setting.

If you do not know what you want specifically, you cannot acquire the necessary steps to achieve it, you will be walking in circles until someone makes a plan for your life, therefore you become the victim of life itself.

Chapter 6. Two of my personal goals

Personally, I was apart of the 90% of people, I set goals in my mind and I would never achieve them, whatever I did I couldn't make anything into reality, my goals were lousy and not exciting, I remember to set a goal as vague as " I just want to make something work in my career" what do you think I got? (Remember a goal has to be specific and enthusiastic) I got what I always got, which was I could not make anything work. Then I turned my life around as I learned about the power of correct goal setting, I can tell you a couple of my goals in different areas of my life.

Immediately I started by writing a financial goal, I wrote that I wanted to make 2000 euros in passive income per month within 1 year(I set a specific date in my personal timeline, which you will learn later in the specific steps of the formula), In Portugal the average income is about 1000 euros, so for a guy that was still in college doubling the average national wage in passive income was a pretty good achievement, and the interesting part was that I didn't stop working until I got my results, it was incredible. You get this amazing feeling of being unstoppable, the excitement kept me energized and doing whatever it took to make it a reality. The level of commitment will drive you towards your goals, along the way you may discover some interesting things, in my case I developed this amazing passion by financial markets and for personal development.

One other goal that I set was about my health, I was eating poorly, not exercising. So I wrote down, I need to have "X" Kg and my body fat percentage has to be "Y" in exactly 6 months, not only I achieve it within 5 months but also I had a different vision of life. You see, there is something about goal setting that the humankind still doesn't fully understand but when you get your subconscious and or conscious mind working together to achieve a specific goal, your mind will do absolutely everything to achieve it, in about a week I knew more about health than I did in my entire life, I devoured books from doctors and nutritionists, I study various courses, I saw hundreds of hours of health content.

Chapter 7. Life Values:

Your river of motivation

Values are simply, what is most important to us, they drive all upfront motivation.

Don't worry, I am not going to get very deep within values.

Let me ask you something, what do you rather have? And you could only pick one.

1) Passion
2) Success
3) Happiness
4) Adventure
5) Love

It's different for everyone, some people value success more than love, others value happiness more than success. Everyone in life learned to take different emotions and give them levels of importance.

Take someone for example that values success and does not value love, this means that if this person had to choose between a business meeting or family, they would choose the business meeting because they value success. And vice-versa, given the same situation, if someone valued love and does not value success, they would've said something along the lines of 'My family is everyting, work comes after'.

So, you have to ask yourself what key values drive you in life?

Are you driven by success, security, freedom, God, friendship, love, power?

Think about this and write down five of the most important values in your life. Ask yourself the following questions, 'What's more important to me in life? Why do I do what I do? What drives me as a person?

Remember should only be emotional states. For example, if you write down 'money', money is not an emotional state, ask yourself, 'what does 'Money' give you? Power, Freedom, security, etc. Same with family.

My Values

1_____

_____

_____

2_____

_____

_____

3_____

_____

_____

4_____

_____

_____

5_____

_____

_____

Ok, great! Once you know what your values are, you know what motivates you unconsciously! You have to use them to drive you towards your goals. This is very important, your values must be aligned with your goals, if this criteria is not met, you would probably procrastinate so much that you eventually give up or don't start at all.

For example, if your goal is to double your income in twelve months, you have to write down all the reasons why this is really important to you. Only if your reasons are aligned to your core values will you be truly driven to achieve them. Here are some powerful reasons that drive people to make their millions... I To feed the poor and do more of God's work. (contribution) I I want to prove to myself and others that I can succeed. (pride) I I want to be the best in my industry. (success) I To give my family members the very best in life. (family) I Doubling my income means doubling the value I create to my customers and the people around me. I will be making a difference to more lives through my work. (contribution) I I will have peace of mind knowing that my family's needs will always be met. (security)

Chapter 8. Designing your future

There are 3 elements you must keep in mind when writing your goals

1- The goal must be specific
2- The goal must be motivating
3- You must write your goals without restrictions, stretch your imagination and your goals, the universe is the limit.

With these three elements in mind, prepare yourself to start writing your path in life, your vision, and your destiny. This exercise is a unique exercise that will help you to tap into your subconscious mind and extract what you really want to achieve/create in the next 10 to 15 years of your life.

Now, one last thing, to help you get better results I need you to actively do the following things:

1- Suspend your internal critic and your judgment in every aspect.

2- Let your imagination loose, like if you were daydreaming

3- Ask yourself 'What would I do if I knew I could not fail?

4- Write with passion and enthusiasm, Ask yourself, ' What would I love to do? What am I passionate about? If I was rich, what would I do and not get paid? If I could create a life full of passion, what would it be?

5- The final one, DON'T STOP WRITING, whatever you do, please do not stop. Do not stop that pen until the time is up

Find a quiet place where you can spend the next 25 to 30 minutes fully engaged in the exercise. Turn your mobile off, shut the door, lock the door if needed.

Get your pen and paper and when your ready, follow the time (use a countdown clock and put in front of you) and write all the goals you want to achieve in the categories of life. Remember the three elements. Be very specific, exciting/motivating, and set quantum goals, put specific deadlines for each goal, deadlines are crucial.

I am going to give you some questions so that you can let your imagination fly.

Are you Ready? I want to write nonstop like if you were to run for your life, never look back, just keep moving forward. KEEP THE PEN MOVING

GO!

personal development (5 mins)

What kind of person do you want to become? What would you like to do? What do you want to learn? What skills do you want to learn? Perhaps playing the piano? Dance the samba? Public speaking? Would you like to sing? What would you like to create? What would be some abilities you want to master? What are some character traits you like to develop? How do you want to feel emotionally about yourself? What are some fears you want to conquer? What would you like to learn about?

Do you want to learn a new language? Do you want to put yourself into a growth path? What are some of your spiritual goals?

How would you want to treat other people? What do you need to do in order to get it? How many books what you like to read in a day, in a month, in a year? What books would you like to read? Would you like to write your own book? What is your ideal weight? What is your strategy to get in shape? Would you like to learn how to invest?

_____

_____

_____

_____

_____

_____

_____

_____

_____

_____

_____

_____

_____

_____

_____

_____

CAREER AND EDUCATIONS ASPIRATIONS (5 MINUTES)

What do you want to accomplish? What type of value would you want to create in your career? What position do you see yourself aiming for? How could you be the best at what you do? Perhaps you want to switch careers? What kind of career do you want? What kind of boss do you want? Do you want to start a business? What kind of business do you want to start? A Marketing business? A real estate business? A construction business? What kind of boss do you want to be? How would you satisfy your costumers? What are the goals you have for your business? Do you want to take your company public? Do you want to franchise your business? What do you want to achieve in sales, shares and profit?

_____

_____

_____

_____

_____

_____

_____

_____

_____

_____

_____

_____

_____

MONEY AND LIFESTYLE (5 Minutes)

How much would you like to earn a week, a month, a year? When and how much do you want to retire with? What are some incomes that you want to create? What specifically do you want? How much would you like to increase your income each year, over the next 5 to 20 years? Do you want to achieve a Million-dollar net worth? Billion dollars? Describe your ideal lifestyle! Do you want a helicopter? Do you want to own your own private airplane? Do you want a beach house? Are there certain places you want to visit? What kind of car do you want? Do you want a Porsche? Ferrari? Lamborghini? Perhaps a Rolls Royce? What is your target annual Return of investments? Do you want a butler or a maid? Do you want to own a castle? Do you want to build a home? Do you want to go to Fiji and swim with the dolphins? Where would you like to go? What kind of house do you want to live in? Do you want to travel the world? Where specifically? Maybe Greece? Fiji Island? Caribbean's? What are other dream luxuries you want to have?

_____

_____

_____

_____

_____

_____

_____

_____

_____

SOCIAL AND FAMILY RELATIONSHIPS (5 Minutes)

who would you like to be close to you?
who would you like to meet personally?
Who do you want to surround yourself with?
What kind of son, daughter, spouse, father, or mother do you want to be?

_____

_____

_____

_____

_____

_____

_____

_____

_____

_____

_____

_____

_____

_____

_____

_____

_____

_____

CONTRIBUTION GOALS (5 Minutes)

What would you like to give in your life?

What are your long-term contribution goals?

Do you want to start a charity? What kind of charity?

Would you like to receive an exchange student?

How would you be able to contribute to your neighborhood, your community, your nation, the world?

Would you like to volunteer to help children?

Do you want to work with the disabled, the troubled teens or to help older people? Would you like to fight for animal rights? Do you want to work with humanitarian agencies around the world?

_____

_____

_____

_____

_____

_____

_____

_____

_____

_____

Alright! Give yourself a tap on the back!

You should have a nice list of all the things you want to create in your life.

Now, in order for you to manifest your goal you MUST take it through the eight-step goal achievement blueprint!

The eight steps will enable you to take the goal written and transform it into real life.

Go through all of your goals and put them into different time frames, One Year, Five Years, Ten Years, and fifteen years (You could do more, it's up to you). Do this on the worksheet below. Remember the deadline is one of the most critical things. Goals are nothing but dreams with deadlines!

Goals within One Year

Personal Development

Goal 1.

Goal_____

_____

Deadline_____

_____

Three Action Steps (24
hours)_____

_____

_____

Goal 2.

Goal_____

_____

Deadline_____

_____

Three Action Steps (24
hours)_____

_____

_____

Goal 3.

Goal_____

_____

Deadline_____

_____

Three Action Steps (24
hours)_____

_____

_____

Goal 4.

Goal_____

_____

Deadline_____

_____

Three Action Steps (24
hours)_____

_____

_____

Career and Educations Aspirations

Goal 1.

Goal_____

_____

Deadline_____

_____

Three Action Steps (24
hours)_____

_____

_____

Goal 2.

Goal_____

_____

Deadline_____

_____

Three Action Steps (24

hours)_____

_____

_____

Goal 3.

Goal_____

_____

Deadline_____

_____

Three Action Steps (24 hours)_____

_____

_____

Goal 4.

Goal_____

_____

Deadline_____

_____

Three Action Steps (24 hours)_____

_____

_____

Money and Lifestyle

Goal 1.

Goal_____

_____

Deadline_____

_____

Three Action Steps (24
hours)_____

_____

_____

Goal 2.

Goal_____

_____

Deadline_____

_____

Three Action Steps (24
hours)_____

_____

_____

Goal 3.

Goal_____

_____

Deadline_____

_____

Three Action Steps (24
hours)_____

_____

_____

<u>Goal 4.</u>

Goal_____

_____

Deadline_____

_____

Three Action Steps (24
hours)_____

_____

_____

<u>Social and Family Relationships</u>

<u>Goal 1.</u>

Goal_____

_____

Deadline_____

_____

Three Action Steps (24 hours)_____

_____

_____

Goal 2.

Goal_____

_____

Deadline_____

_____

Three Action Steps (24 hours)_____

_____

_____

Goal 3.

Goal_____

_____

Deadline_____

_____

Three Action Steps (24
hours)_____

_____

_____

Goal 4.

Goal_____

_____

Deadline_____

_____

Three Action Steps (24
hours)_____

_____

_____

Contribution Goals

Goal 1.

Goal_____

_____

Deadline_____

_____

Three Action Steps (24
hours)_____

_____

_____

Goal 2.

Goal_____

_____

Deadline_____

_____

Three Action Steps (24 hours)_____

_____

_____

Goal 3.

Goal_____

_____

Deadline_____

_____

Three Action Steps (24 hours)_____

_____

_____

Goal 4.

Goal_____

_____

Deadline_____

_____

Three Action Steps (24 hours)_____

_____

_____

The first thing to do is to get the benefits from the momentum, I am a big believer in momentum. Take this 24-hour challenge.

When we start taking the first steps towards a goal, we create momentum, momentum is this powerful tool that we can utilize in our favor. Doesn't matter if the goal needs to be accomplished within one year or twenty years, we take three steps, and there are always three steps you can take, if you wanted to buy a new car and you didn't have the money to buy it, you could take a test drive (first action), you could call the dealer and tell them to send a brochure (second action) and you could pre-order the car (third action). I found out that the best way is to make a public commitment to other people or something that involves committing some money (don't go overboard here). By doing this, you are telling yourself and your brain that you are serious and committed to achieve this goal.

Another example, if you wanted to lose weight, you could go to your local gym and pay 6 months advanced or you could give away all your clothes and go out and replace it with a wardrobe three sizes smaller!

Goals within Five Years

<u>Personal Development</u>

<u>Goal 1.</u>

Goal_____

_____

Deadline_____

_____

<u>Goal 2.</u>

Goal_____

_____

Deadline_____

_____

Goal 3.

Goal_____

_____

Deadline_____

_____

Goal 4.

Goal_____

_____

Deadline_____

_____

Career and Educations Aspirations

Goal 1.

Goal_____

_____

Deadline_____

_____

Goal 2.

Goal_____

_____

Deadline_____

_____

Goal 3.

Goal_____

_____

Deadline_____

_____

Goal 4.

Goal_____

_____

Deadline_____

_____

Money and Lifestyle

Goal 1.

Goal_____

_____

Deadline_____

_____

Goal 2.

Goal_____

_____

Deadline_____

_____

Goal 3.

Goal_____

_____

Deadline_____

_____

Goal 4.

Goal_____

_____

Deadline_____

_____

Social and Family Relationships

Goal 1.

Goal_____

_____

Deadline_____

_____

Goal 2.

Goal_____

_____

Deadline_____

_____

Goal 3.

Goal_____

_____

Deadline_____

_____

Goal 4.

Goal_____

_____

Deadline_____

_____

Contribution Goals

Goal 1.

Goal_____

_____

Deadline_____

_____

Goal 2.

Goal_____

_____

Deadline_____

_____

Goal 3.

Goal_____

_____

Deadline_____

_____

Goal 4.

Goal_____

_____

Deadline_____

_____

Goals within Ten Years

Personal Development

Goal 1.

Goal_____

_____

Deadline_____

_____

Goal 2.

Goal_____

_____

Deadline_____

_____

Goal 3.

Goal_____

_____

Deadline_____

_____

Goal 4.

Goal_____

_____

Deadline_____

_____

Career and Educations Aspirations

Goal 1.

Goal_____

_____

Deadline_____

_____

Goal 2.

Goal_____

_____

Deadline_____

_____

Goal 3.

Goal_____

_____

Deadline_____

_____

Goal 4.

Goal_____

_____

Deadline_____

_____

Money and Lifestyle

Goal 1.

Goal_____

_____

Deadline_____

_____

Goal 2.

Goal_____

_____

Deadline_____

_____

Goal 3.

Goal_____

_____

Deadline_____

_____

Goal 4.

Goal_____

_____

Deadline_____

_____

Social and Family Relationships

Goal 1.

Goal_____

_____

Deadline_____

_____

Goal 2.

Goal_____

_____

Deadline_____

_____

<u>Goal 3.</u>

Goal_____

_____

Deadline_____

_____

<u>Goal 4.</u>

Goal_____

_____

Deadline_____

_____

Contribution Goals

Goal 1.

Goal_____

_____

Deadline_____

_____

Goal 2.

Goal_____

_____

Deadline_____

_____

Goal 3.

Goal_____

_____

Deadline_____

_____

Goal 4.

Goal_____

_____

Deadline_____

_____

Goals within Fifteen Years

Personal Development

Goal 1.

Goal_____

_____

Deadline_____

_____

Goal 2.

Goal_____

_____

Deadline_____

_____

Goal 3.

Goal_____

_____

Deadline_____

_____

Goal 4.

Goal_____

_____

Deadline_____

_____

Career and Educations Aspirations

Goal 1.

Goal_____

_____

Deadline_____

_____

Goal 2.

Goal_____

_____

Deadline_____

_____

Goal 3.

Goal_____

_____

Deadline_____

_____

Goal 4.

Goal_____

_____

Deadline_____

_____

Money and Lifestyle

Goal 1.

Goal_____

_____

Deadline_____

_____

Goal 2.

Goal_____

_____

Deadline_____

_____

Goal 3.

Goal_____

_____

Deadline_____

_____

Goal 4.

Goal_____

_____

Deadline_____

_____

Social and Family Relationships

Goal 1.

Goal_____

_____

Deadline_____

_____

Goal 2.

Goal_____

_____

Deadline_____

_____

Goal 3.

Goal_____

_____

Deadline_____

_____

Goal 4.

Goal_____

_____

Deadline_____

_____

Contribution Goals

Goal 1.

Goal_____

_____

Deadline_____

_____

Goal 2.

Goal_____

_____

Deadline_____

_____

Goal 3.

Goal_____

_____

Deadline_____

_____

Goal 4.

Goal_____

_____

Deadline_____

_____

The next step is to take your major one-year
goals and put them through the eight-step goal
achievement blueprint.

Chapter 9. Eight-Step

Goal Achievement

Blueprint

Step 1- What do you want? Give specific details and what is the deadline?

_____

_____

_____

_____

Step 2- Make a research and find a model of excellence. (Remember the four steps of modeling)

_____

_____

_____

_____

Step 3 – What specific actions and requirements do you need to arrive at your goal? What are the deadlines?

_____

_____

_____

_____

Step 4 – What resources do you need? (Money, talent, People, Skills)

_____

_____

_____

_____

Step 5 – What are 3 action steps to take? You want to get the best of momentum, remember, you have a limit of 24 hours.

_____

_____

_____

_____

Step 6 – Schedule this in your organizer, every goal with deadlines, and the 3 action steps!

Step 7 – Why must you achieve this goal?

Step 8 – Visualize the goal every day (Bellow I am going to give you a technique that puts this goal into your timeline so that it occurs in your unconscious mind).

The **'why'** is much more important than the 'how'. When you know why you want something, your brain will automatically find new paths even when the odds are against you.

We must have enough compelling reasons to drive us forward to do whatever it takes to achieve our goals. Remember, Purpose is stronger than outcome.

Your 'why' must be in line with your values.

Why is it important for you to achieve this goal?

_____

_____

_____

_____

_____

_____

_____

_____

Visualize your goal

What drives our actions is not logic but the emotional states that we are in. Visualizing your goals will put you in peak performance so that you can always make the best decisions, if you don't visualize your goal daily, you will keep putting it off. Personally, in the beginning I do it two times a day (in the morning and before I go to sleep). Take your major goals and visualize yourself in the future already achieving it.

Firs run your goal through this formula:

It is now _____ (Future date), I am/I have

_____

(End step or 'what is the final thing that has to happen for you to know you reach your goal?')

I am going to give you an example, which was one of my goals.

It is now June First, 2019. I am looking at my past three months bank statement and I see that my income is 2000 euros a month in passive income.

Once you have written this formula, I want you to start visualizing this goal! First read all of the steps and then close your eyes and imagine.

Visualization Process

Step 1- Imagine stepping inside the end step (the final thing that has to happen for you to know you reached your goal), looking through your own eyes, hearing the sounds around you, and feeling the feelings of being right there inside the goal.

Step 2- Adjust the quality of the pictures (think of these like a turning knob to increase the level of excitement and motivation), if your imagining a black & white picture, change it to color and notice if that affects the feelings in your own body. if it's a still picture, change it, add some movement, Put the picture centered! If it is dim, make it brighter. Make it bigger.

Step 3- Adjust the quality of the sounds, if you are hearing the sounds in mono, make it stereo. Make it louder and make the sounds in a high pitch.

Step 4 – Adjust the quality of what you say to yourself. If you are saying it in mono, change it to stereo, add some excitement in what you say.

Step 5 – Adjust the quality of your feelings, if you start to feel some feelings, locate them, and make it bigger.

Step 6 – imagine stepping out of the picture but you are going to leave your body in the picture so that you can see yourself in it, like if you were seeing a movie.

Step 7 – Imagine taking that picture in your hands and rise above your timeline (you can do this by asking yourself, 'where does the past is in relation to my body? Physically point. Then ask yourself 'where does the future is in relation to my body? Trust you unconscious), you see yourself above Now, the past is in one direction and the future in another.

Step 8 – Imagine floating to your future (always above it) and find yourself above the date where you said the event would happen.

Step 9 – Drop the picture down into the stream of time bellow and notice that it takes the place of the date you said that would occur. Look back towards the now and notice everything that had to happen to lead up to that event, then look towards the future and notice that the future changes, this was only the beginning, the future is brighter.

Step 10 – Come all the way back to now, and back to the room.

Start visualizing your goals today.

Usually this is the part of goal-setting that people dislike because it requires work to accomplish them.

Remember what I said in the beginning of the book, only you can change your life. If you want to succeed with effective goal setting, you need to know what's important throughout all areas of life. Remember, if you don't have a plan, a vision, you will end up in circles.

Goals require patient, dedication, persistence, and faith. So, don't let your future be in the hands of someone else, take full responsibility for your life and start designing your life.

Chapter 10. The Deadly Sins Of Goal Setting

Sin 1. Not knowing what you want

People will often tell me that they don't know what they want, or they don't know what's the highway to take. Meanwhile they don't know how much time they are wasting, choose a path, take massive action, and don't question it. Let me ask your something, 'How much time did you lose by not knowing what you want?' more than you wanted, right? One other reality check, you cannot buy time, time is limited. The day you are born you have a limited amount of time to live, so do not waste it, make the best out of your time.

It's crucial that our goals are personal and meaningful; otherwise, we'd have no reason to work towards them. In other words, the reasons 'why' we want to reach our goals are always going to be more important than 'what' we ever want to achieve. Consider the big goal of 'getting rich'. This goal will be completely meaningless to

Sin 2. Not Writing Goals Down

As I explained in the early section of the book, people who write down their goals have a higher chance of achieving it. The most efficient way to reinforce a new key concept you learn and a long-term commitment to your goals is to write them down and visualize the goals daily.

Sin 3. Having Unclear Motivations

The reasons 'why' we want to reach our goals are always going to be more important than 'what' we want to achieve.

For example, if your goal is to get rich, but if you don't have a strong enough 'why' this goal will be meaningless which is reinforced by your values.

If your reason for making more money is just to buy more things or to fuel your spending habits, you might find it difficult to be authentically motivated by this.

If your reason is to pay for your kid's college or to live a secure life, where everyone in your family doesn't have to worry about paying their bills, you will most likely feel more excited, more passionate and the dream turns into reality

Whatever your underlying reasons are for doing what you want to do, they will all be important reasons, as they're directly personal to you.

Sin 4. Having limiting beliefs

One of the worst feelings is thinking that you can't achieve something or its impossible, these are nothing more than limiting beliefs. Many people dream about what they would love to have, when it comes to committing to a specific plan their brain just goes 'no way', 'too much work'. Unless we break free from limiting beliefs, we will never dare to go for it.

Sin 5. Not Having a Strategy

After knowing what you want, you need how to get there, having a strategy is the highway to your goal. Having a written goal is just the beginning, you need an action plan that directs you towards achieving your goal or your end step.

Every person who Is an achiever needs to have a well-written plan, the best way is to enjoy the process. You can use modeling to accelerate the process, remember, if you model someone, you will think, behave, and act like them, you will produce the same results.

Sin 6. Not Taking Consistent Action

I can tell you that I am not smarter than everybody else, Bill Gates, Richard Branson, Tony Robbins are not smarter than everybody else, they just take consistent action and they produce certain results. Although your strategy will guide you and keep you right on what to do, you're still going to have a lot of barriers, people getting mad at you, business plans failing, and many others, but you got to resist and keep taking consistent action.

Sometimes life changes its course, and this is common for everyone, so don't be concerned if you need to make changes as you go or even start the goal-setting process all over again.

Sin 7. Losing Focus

Achieving your goals requires patience, dedication, persistence, and faith. You will lose focus on the way, but it's extremely important no to quit, try getting it into your conscious so that when you notice that you are losing focus, break that pattern and refocus. To help you, try telling a trusted friend or someone you trust to support you throughout the process.

About The Author

Alex Silva is the author of The Goal Setting Workshop. He lives in Leiria, Portugal. Alex loves educating and inspiring other authors and entrepreneurs to succeed and live the life of their dreams.

Learn more about Alex at www.thealexsilva.com

Learn more about Alex at amazon.com/author/thealexsilva

One Last Thing…

If you enjoyed this book or found it useful I'd be very grateful if you'd post a short review on Amazon. Your support really does make a difference and I read all the reviews personally so I can get your feedback and make this book even better.

Thanks again for your support!

www.ingramcontent.com/pod-product-compliance
Lightning Source LLC
Chambersburg PA
CBHW020547220526
45463CB00006B/2215